LIFE HACKING SPIRITUAL DISCIPLINES

LIFE HACKING SPIRITUAL DISCIPLINES

HOW TO FIND
GOD
IN A NOISY WORLD

JOE FONTENOT

Five Round Rocks Media, LLC
New Orleans

First Five Round Rocks Media hardback edition 2016
First Five Round Rocks Media paperback edition 2016
First Five Round Rocks Media ebook edition 2016
ISBN 978-0-9981007-2-2 (hardback)
ISBN 978-0-9981007-0-8 (paperback)
ISBN 978-0-9981007-1-5 (ebook)

Published by Five Round Rocks Media, LLC
www.FiveRoundRocks.com

for Kristin,
who puts up with me, and puts up with me, and
puts up with me…

CONTENTS

*Conforming to a religious subculture
is simply not a compelling enough vision
to captivate the human spirit.*

It was not intended to be.

- John Ortberg

A MANIFESTO...SORT OF

"I'm not smart,
but I like to observe.
Millions saw the apple fall,
but Newton was the one who asked why."
- William Hazlitt

This book is not about studying the spiritual disciplines. It's about implementing them.

I believe that the majority of Christians in the West suffer from superficiality, and the world sees this. *We* see this. It comes out in gossip and in a constant focus on our own image instead of God's image. And when the statistics come out, there's no difference between those living for God and those living for themselves. If we're truly a changed people—rejuvenated and reborn, then let's prove it. After all, that's how Jesus said people would recognize us (see John 8 for more on that).

So more than anything else, this little book is a manifesto.

I didn't want to call it that, because manifestos are a bit cliché these days. And this probably has a bit more research than the average manifesto. So, it's a quasi-manifesto. But either way, the point is the same. Until we make this spiritual focus a part of our daily lives, we won't get traction.

But there's a key to all of this. I think about my friend who bench presses over 400 pounds. That's more than two of me. But he didn't get to be like that simply because he wanted it, and he also didn't get there because he merely had the potential. He got there because he goes to the gym *every day.*

And that's how our spiritual lives work as well. We're not going to understand God better until we put in the time to get to know Him. And we're not going to understand what he's carved out specifically for us in this life until we know Him and have learned how to hear His voice.

If you're new to all of this, and you've never had a regular time of prayer and Bible reading, then this book is for you. And if you're an old soul at this, but struggle with keeping it consistent, then this book is also for you. In the end, this is a practical book designed to give anyone who desires to learn more the basic tools needed.

But I'm not writing here about the spiritual disciplines themselves. With time, those will come. They are a natural outworking of spending time with God, and there are many great books on that subject already. Instead, this short book is about the *first step*. It's about *how* you get there.

The term "Life hacking" is a relatively new one. It comes out of the computer world and refers to a technique that makes a process easier or faster. In other words, it's a solution. When tech writer Danny O'Brien first used the term, he was referring to routines that efficient programmers implemented. "Hacks are often a way of cutting through an apparently complex system with a really simple, nonobvious [sic] fix."[1] When laid bare, these are the things that separate the high performers from the rest.

The Spiritual Disciplines, on the other hand, are habits, behaviors, and routines designed to re-focus ourselves on the things of God. Take for example fasting. Fasting is just as much a matter of physical self-control as it is spiritual self-control. We restrain our bodies from food so that we can redirect our spirits toward God.

And so if we don't have the basic disciplines of carving out a few minutes a day to read God's Word and hear from Him—a time when we're 100 percent present—then we'll never be able to jump into the big waters of faith that we read about in the New Testament and have seen in the lives of spiritual giants down through the ages.

David Platt wrote a wonderfully revolutionary book called *Radical*. And to most people—myself included—it *was* radical. Its entire premise is that the American dream *just might not* be what Jesus had in mind when he was saying things like "take up your cross and follow me." These outside-the-box perspectives are needed. While I can't say enough good about Platt and his work, a flash of inspiration is not going to change most of us. Not in the long run. Just like we can't construct buildings or establish careers in a day, neither can we radically transform our lives in an instance of inspiration (or guilt). Instead, what *will* change us—and what's been proven to change us—is summed up in a single word. It's what the Japanese call *kaizen*.

After World War II Dr. W. Edwards Deming introduced the Japanese to the secret of American success. It has since become ingrained in their cultural thinking, making companies like Toyota the top in their industry. During WWII when America was ramping up production to support her forces overseas, needed supplies started to become scarce. So what did America do? She focused on refining processes to become more efficient, and she started using the best quality products because they broke less and paid off more in the long term. It was just as much a focus on the process as it was the product. After the war, America relaxed her focus, but the Japanese never did. They continued to implement *kaizen* and over time little companies like Toyota and Sony became worldwide industry leaders. In short, *kaizen* is not one thing, but many things. It not a giant leap, but a thousand tiny steps. However, not just any steps will do, they must be the *right* steps.

Understanding this is what it takes to have a successful spiritual life.

The right steps aren't hard. They're not a choreographed dance, or a tight-rope walk—those are things for the professionals. The steps themselves are simple, just as simple as walking itself. After a while, you forget how you do it and it's all natural. But at first it's not. At first you have to focus on it. My youngest, who turned one a few months ago still randomly falls over when she's walking. It's kind of funny to watch. The whole walking process isn't quite natural to her yet. But it'll come. And so it is for us and our spiritual walk. It's always a rough start, but success is given to those who keep at it.

ALL THE RIGHT STEPS

So what do the steps to a successful spiritual life look like?

Simply this: every day, meet with God.

That's it.

Each day is another step.

The journey seems impossibly far at the outset. And when your perspective shows you only what you don't have, the journey *is* indeed long. Too long. But with God, we know the destination is His. That's His job, and we don't have to worry about it. If we're coming to Him honestly each day, the fruit of that relationship will appear. Our job is to focus on the walk, the *doing* of it each day. And this is when the spiritual disciplines come alive.

It's here that the Scripture becomes acutely relevant to our daily lives. It's here that we enter His throne room, tripping over ourselves in awe. And it's here where we find ourselves doubled over in thanksgiving for all the undeserved gifts He's given us. These mountain-top moments aren't meant to be rare moments—God intends for them to be part of our *daily* life. Because experiencing

God *is* that good. But to get there, we have to spend regular time *with* God.

This regular time with God is the right steps to a full and meaningful life.

LEARNING TO FIND GOD IN A NOISY WORLD

There are many spiritual disciplines. But throughout this book, I mostly reference these two: prayer and reading God's Word. The reason is not that the others are unimportant, but that the others are made easier by first focusing on these. In many ways, prayer and Bible reading are the foundational disciplines.

Prayer embodies the *relationship* we have with God. In the book of James, James writes that merely *believing* God exists is not sufficient to have a healthy relationship with Him. In fact, it's as if He implies that believing is only entrance to the game, for "even the *demons* believe."[2] But Jesus, even with His busy schedule, made prayer a priority. So much so that he would occasionally forgo sleep and other ministry needs, focusing instead on prayer. This is because, like nothing else, prayer deepens our relationship with our Father. It sets our emotional tones and refocuses our minds to what matters most: God's Kingdom.[3]

The second discipline, reading God's Word, forms the objective backbone to the rest of our lives. Like a steady stream of knowledge, it informs our prayers and builds the rest of our worldview. While prayer tends to be subjective, God's Word is steady and unchanging. And in those difficult times when God seems far away and our prayers seem empty, God's Word is still solidly the same. The two disciplines work as a combination, making a base for our spiritual formation. Once prayer and God's Word become ingrained in our thought process, moving on to other disciplines becomes natural.

There is no authoritative list of spiritual disciplines. As I mentioned above, the spiritual disciplines are what help us re-focus our attention on God. Because of this, they include (in no particular order) fasting, service, worship, confession, solitude, submission, study, prayer, meditation, and simplicity.[4] As you read this book, you'll notice that some of these become supporting disciplines for the others, while others are used in tandem. The point with the spiritual disciplines is that they cause our minds and bodies and souls to be re-focused on God. If that's happening, then you're doing them right.

THE REST OF THIS BOOK

The rest of this book is about understanding our own wiring. What does it take to make this daily time happen? If you're like me, you've spent more time than you have the courage to admit trying and failing...but mostly failing.

My own journey into this started in frustration for what should be simple. *Just wake up early and do it.*

But it wasn't until I understood (what now seems so basic and simple) that I actually gained traction in making my daily time with God consistent. It wasn't until I understood the way God's wired us, as whole beings. All the areas of our life are like a spider's web. If you pull on one end, the other side feels the tug. And so I didn't begin to gain long-term traction in my daily time with God until I started thinking holistically.

Showing you how to do that is what this little book is about.

Chapter One looks at how God's wired our brains. Understanding how we're wired goes a long way toward understanding how to *use* that wiring.

Chapter Two is about understanding what it takes to make new habits and break old ones. It's estimated between 30 and 40 percent of what we do is habit—that's a big part of our lives. Making lasting change comes from having good habits.

Chapter Three looks at willpower and the myths surrounding it. Willpower is indeed powerful…if we use it how it's designed. However, most of the time we use it for something else entirely, and our changes fall flat. There's a smarter way.

Chapter Four is about focus. When you finally get to the point of sitting down to pray, why is it so hard to concentrate? Am I just not good at focusing, or am I missing something? But focus is also about something deeper—here we look at what constitutes true learning.

In **Chapter Five,** your body conspires against you. Or, perhaps, what you're *doing* with your body is making a big difference in how successful you are at creating a daily prayer habit. This is as much a way of thinking as it is a way of acting.

Finally, **Chapter Six** is about putting the external parts in place to be like bumpers to your bowling ball. In bowling, bumpers are kind of like cheating. All you need to do is toss the ball hard enough and you'll make it. But in life, bumpers are the support group that keeps us on the rails.

HARD TIMES, GOOD TIMES

One more quick note. In my life, I've had hard times and I've had good times.

During the hard times, these life hacks aren't as necessary. Our souls are raw and we are naturally drawn to desire healing and comfort.[5] However, it is often during the *good* times that we struggle the most with wanting God. To echo words Paul wrote two millennia ago: "I don't understand myself at all, for I really want to do what is right, but I can't. I do what I don't want to—what I hate" (Romans 7:15, TLB).

So, it is to the good times we now turn, to better learn how to do what we really want to do.

And if you find that this book helped bring you closer to that place, please take a second to leave a review on Amazon.

That helps me make the next book better, and it helps other readers find what they're looking for. So really, your review is making us all better. :)

Now, on to the life hacks for spiritual disciplines.

NOTES

[1] http://lifehacker.com/036370/interview-father-of-life-hacks-danny-obrien, accessed 6/12/16.

[2] James 2:19, emphasis added.

[3] In response to our (legitimate) needs, Jesus teaches us to keep our first focus on the Kingdom, promising that God will take care of the rest (Matthew 6:33).

[4] Richard Foster in his book *Celebration of Disciplines* expands this list further. It is a highly recommended read.

[5] It's also true we don't always desire *God*. This can be due to anger, or something else entirely. But the point remains the same: an established routine will often help us bypass some of our own reluctance, giving us an often much-needed leg up.

chapter one

YOU AND YOUR BRAIN

"Working hard and working smart can sometimes be two different things."
- Byron Dorgan

"It doesn't matter how beautiful your theory is…
If it doesn't agree with experiment, it's wrong."
- Richard Feynman

AM I CHEATING?

Is using physical practices to improve our spiritual relationship with God cheating? In other words, is it any *less* spiritual to incorporate non-spiritual routines in my prayer and devotion time?

I think not.

In fact, I'd go as far as saying it's finally playing by the rules.

When God created the first man and woman, He did it in both perfect unity with Himself and with the rest of His created world. That picture of unity includes both the spiritual *and* the physical. After the Fall, after sin crept into every part of our lives, our physical and spiritual selves became stunted. Our bodies began dying, and our spirits were separated from God.

Much of what Jesus taught was to help us understand what we've long since forgotten. When talking about proper worship, he said plainly we are to love God with our hearts, souls, and minds (Matthew 22:37). New Testament scholar William Hendriksen notes that these are not specific compartments, but represent our thoughts, emotions, and attitude.[1] In other words, Jesus was referencing our whole selves. All of our being should be devoted to God.

The premise of this short book is that we are much more successful in developing spiritual disciplines—and with them, spiritual maturity—when we see ourselves *holistically*. It's not always your lack of devotion that keeps you from pulling an all-nighter in prayer. Just like it's not your lack of desire that keeps you from running a full marathon without ever having trained. These are big things, and they require deliberate training and preparation.

The rest of this book will look at what it takes to create a regular time with God. From this regular time flows the richness and purpose of a life following God.

But to do that, we first need to understand how our brains work. And perhaps the best way to do that is to start with porn.

PORN IS AS PORN DOES

Porn? Yes, porn.

Do you know why porn is so addictive? It's a combination of two powerful things. The first is the intimacy of sex. God made sex to allow two people to bond in a way that is fundamentally different from any other relationship.

The second factor is how the brain itself works. And it's this part that directly affects our habits and behaviors.

Each time the brain does something, a neural pathway is created. When an action is repeated over and over, the path gets worn and established. Eventually neural highways form, and the brain begins *automatically* routing thoughts through these highways. William M. Struthers, professor of psychology at Wheaton College, in his book *Wired For Intimacy*, writes:

> The neural circuitry anchors this process solidly in the brain. With each lingering stare, pornography deepens a Grand Canyon-like gorge in the brain through which images of women are destined to flow. This extends to women that they have not seen naked or engaging in sexual acts as well. All women become potential porn stars in the minds of these men. They have unknowingly created a neurological circuit that imprisons their ability to see women rightly as created in God's image.[2]

Porn illustrates openly and dangerously the power of our neural wiring. Our brains are made for efficiency and routine. And our brains are especially rewarding to strong things. Like sex. And chocolate. And pretty much anything we feel intensely about, be it good or bad.

By the time we become adults, some of our neural pathways have become so ingrained that we aren't even aware of them anymore. They've become buried in our subconscious, acting as invisible guideposts to everything we do. Most of us refer to this as "common sense." For instance, we don't have to think about the dangers of crossing the street. As soon as we get close to it, our eyes automatically begin scanning for cars that might cream us. In many ways—like for the purpose of staying alive—this common sense (neural automation) is a good thing.

But when we're trying to change certain behaviors, reaching into our subconscious to dig out these streams of automation can be hard. Interestingly, it's author Stephen King who provides us with good advice here.

THE BOYS IN THE BASEMENT

I've never read any of Stephen King's novels. Nothing against Steve, just not my thing. But a few years back, he wrote a nonfiction book called *On Writing*. It's half memoir, half writing advice. And of the dozens of books and hundreds of articles I've read on the craft of writing, his easily pulls rank on the rest. It's top-shelf stuff.

In it he talks about a concept that's come to be known as the "the boys in the basement." Steven Pressfield has called this same concept "the muse."[3] The idea is not mystical, though some treat it that way. It's just a romantic description of how our subconscious minds work.

Our subconscious thoughts are the backbone of our conscious thoughts. As neuroscientist David Eagleman writes, "when an idea is served up from behind the scenes, your neural circuitry has been working on it for hours or days or years, consolidating information and trying out new combinations."[4] This is how, Eagleman explains, you can "notice your name spoken in a conversation across the room that you thought you weren't listening to" or have "a 'hunch' about which choice you should make." It's because your subconscious is constantly working. And it's the work of the subconscious that's largely responsible for what we do.

But this doesn't mean that we (our conscious selves) have no say in the matter. We are still responsible for what both our conscious and subconscious brains do. It's much like the digestive system of the body. Your body will do its best to digest the food you eat. And depending on that food, you'll be healthy or unhealthy. Just because the digestion process is automatic does not mean you're free of responsibility for what you put in your mouth.

And so it with our brains. What we put in will largely be what comes out. But it's not only *what* we put in. It's *how* we put it in.

TO USE THE MUSE

In his book on the subconscious mind, Leonard Mlodinow found that only a tiny part of our brain activity is taken up by our conscious minds. The rest is in our subconscious. "Some scientists estimate that we are conscious of only about 5 percent of our cognitive function." And "deep concentration," continues Mlodinow, "causes the energy consumption in your brain to go up by only about 1 percent."[5] These conclusions are striking if for no other reason than to show that we really are a product of our own wiring and inputs. While that wiring can be changed over time, it's not something that we can do on a whim. Instead, it's something we have to cultivate and build into our lives.

This is relevant when we reconsider the battle cry of change that books like Platt's *Radical* (which, I want to reiterate, is truly a wonderful book) preach. As much as we might be charged up in the moment, or the day, or even the week, unless we make *deeper* structural changes, the fire will fizzle.

But this concept is nothing new. In fact, though presented in different ways, it's become the cornerstone of success and perseverance.

Take for example the religious leaders of Jesus' day. They were obsessed with all kinds of legalism. One such form came in legislating what people could and couldn't eat. In a direct challenge to their authority, Jesus said that what really makes us dirty or clean is not what goes in but what comes *out*. His point was: what goes in is just biology, but what comes out—our words and our actions—is a reflection of our deeper selves (Matthew 15:10-20).

Centuries before Jesus' ministry, God gave the Israelites the same lesson, writing it into his very law. *Be holy as I am holy*, He commanded (Leviticus 20:26).

In Leviticus, God prepared His children to understand the correct way before they would misstep, while in the Gospels Jesus was addressing the problem after it had already been happening.

And the lesson for us all is the same: what we do has an implicit influence on what we think, which in turn drives our future actions.

When I was young, I didn't like school. I loved learning, but my imagination, which fueled so much of that, had a hard time fitting into the structure of the classroom. As a result, I'd get Cs all the time. After a regular pattern of Cs, this became normal. Cs were the kind of grade I got. When I took a test, I just expected I'd get a C.

In that sea of Cs something subtle was happening. I saw the same thing so many times my view of it switched from descriptive to prescriptive. I no longer saw Cs as something I had in the past, but as something I *would be getting* in the future. This is the value of correct thinking.

Scott Adams is the mind and pencil behind the Dilbert comics. In his career-memoir *How to Fail at Almost Everything and Still Win Big,* he talks about what he calls affirmations. These are little sayings he tells himself with the expectation that the repetition will allow them to work themselves into his life. For instance, before he became a world-famous cartoonist, he told himself "I, Scott Adams, will be a famous cartoonist."[6] The statement itself changed nothing. It was only through hard work and relentless persistence that he actually turned comics into a career. But the statement served as a masthead—a compass of encouragement. His affirmation became a reminder of where he wanted to go.

In all of these cases—Jesus and the religious leaders, God guiding His people, my middle-school report card, and Dilbert the comic—the principle is the same: repetition of thought plays a big role in what we actually do. The muse is not another person—it's you. But more specifically, it's a *result* of you. You can't control the muse on a whim, instead, it is the outworking of what you do over and over again.

Learning spiritual disciplines works in quite the same way. It's through repetition and regularity that these things eventually begin to seep out of us. At first it's a struggle. Everything is intentional. But with time—often catching us by surprise—these things begin to become second-nature.

NOTES

[1] Hendricksen, William, *Exposition of the Gospel According to Matthew* (Baker Book House, 1973), 809.

[2] Struthers, William, *Wired For Intimacy* (InterVarsity Press, 2009), 85.

[3] Pressfield, Steven, *The War of Art* (Black Irish Entertainment, 2012).

[4] Eagleman, David, *Incognito* (Pantheon Books, 2011), 7.

[5] Mlodinow, Leonard, *Subliminal* (Random House, 2012) 34-35.

[6] Adams, Scott, *How to Fail at Almost Everything and Still Win Big* (Penguin Group, 2013) 157.

chapter two

IT'S ALL IN THE HABIT

"Your whole life has the same shape of a single day."
- Michael Crichton

I f it promises 21 days to form a successful habit—
it's probably wrong.

Sorry.

The 21-days myth became popular in the 1960s and has since been used to claim everything from losing weight to quitting smoking. As I'm writing this, there are still quite a few titles on Amazon promising to show you how to lose weight,[1] become creative,[2] and—my favorite—*reprogram your genes* (I actually considered buying that last one).[3] But fortunately, research (and common sense) is beginning to catch up to pop culture on this matter, and these myths aren't as common anymore.

In his book *Making Habits, Breaking Habits,* psychologist Jeremy Dean notes a study by the University College in London which found that "on average…it took 66 days until a habit was formed," and in at least one case, the habit was still not formed after 84 days.[4]

The biggest variable in getting a habit started came from how difficult the habit behavior was. People who wanted to eat a piece of fruit every day, for instance, took about 40 days to turn it into a habit. But, to the credit of the 21-day myth, people who only wanted to drink a glass of water after breakfast each morning were able to do it in 20 days or less. (The guy who didn't form a habit in 84 days was trying to do 50 sit-ups each day.)

Dean concludes: "21 days to form a habit is probably right, as long as all you want to do is drink a glass of water after breakfast." While this particular study only lasted 84 days, extrapolating the data, some habits could have taken over eight months to form. That's a lot longer than the popular three-week promise.

This might seem like gloomy news for the habit front, but it's actually not. What it tells us is that if something's not working, it might be because you're giving up too early, or you're going about it wrong, or some combination.

In this chapter we're applying current habit research and what we know about behavioral change to see what it takes to establish a daily prayer time. The theme in all of it? Successful habit formation comes from making *small* changes in the *right* places. (Remember *kaizen* from the Introduction?)

The value of small changes is that we can all do them. They don't require Herculean strength to apply, and by their nature (small) they don't make a big impact on our schedules.

But just because they're small doesn't mean these actions will actually turn into a habit. They have to be done in the *right* places and at the *right* time. It's this combination that makes habits stick.

First, let's look at how a habit actually works.

THREE COMPONENTS OF A HABIT

A habit is made up of three basic components: a cue, a routine, and a reward. What we think of as the habit is the middle part, the routine. But the key to establishing, changing, and breaking habits revolves around the first and the third components: the cue and the reward. Understanding how this works is critical to changing behavior.

CUE

A cue is the trigger that tells your brain to begin the routine. In his *New York Times* bestselling book *The Power of Habit*, Charles Duhigg recognized that his mid-afternoon cookie addiction was triggered, or cued, by boredom. So when he got the urge to eat a cookie, he instead walked around and talked to his cubical neighbors. As it turns out, his brain didn't need the hit of sugar, it just needed some sort of stimulation. Sugar was doing it previously, but when he swapped it out for social interaction, he found his need being met just fine.

So the cue is the event or time of day that tips your brain to start moving down that pre-set neural highway, and doing the habit, or routine.

ROUTINE

The routine is the habit action itself. In Duhigg's above example, the cookie and chatting with coworkers was the routine. Most of our habit-change energy is focused on the routine—the specific action we call the habit—because that's the most obvious part, and that's the part we want to change. But, as we'll see, this is perhaps the hardest way to change a habit. It's the hardest—and often most unsuccessful—because it relies too heavily on willpower

(more on willpower in the next chapter). While a changed routine is the end result, it's often how our cues and rewards work together to that make that happen.

REWARD

This last component, the reward, is how your brain knows the whole thing was worth it. This is the evaluative part. If you ate the cookie, your brain will feel stimulated after the sugar rush and log that as mission-accomplished. Then, the next time the cue happens, your brain will remember the last reward (associating the positive nature of the sugar rush) and want to do it all again. And from this a cycle is formed. But the opposite is also true. If the reward goes unmet, then the next time your brain sees the cue, it's going to push the pass button and move on.

***

A good way to think of how these three parts work together is like a hot dish in an oven. When the timer goes off, you reach in to take it out. The goal is to get the dish from the oven to the counter. But if you think *only* about the dish and reach in with your bare hands, you'll drop the dish and burn your hands.

Instead, you reach in with kitchen mittens or pot holders—something that will insulate your hands. By focusing first on your hands, they can do their job—taking the dish out of the oven.

The pot holders are a bit like a cue and reward. When used properly, they deliver a successful routine (the dish).

The cue is where it all starts. So let's look at how to recognize *existing* cues, and then how to create new ones.

FINDING CUES

The cue is the urge that sets your habit in motion. But somewhat paradoxically *finding* the cue is not always easy.

The key is to pay attention to what's going on at the moment. Charles Duhigg (the guy with the cookie) provides a good framework for doing this. He suggests five questions to ask yourself. Once you feel the urge to do the habit (whether you did it or resisted it) answer these five basic questions: where, when, how, who, and what.

Where: where are you?

When: what time is it?

How: what's your emotional state?

Who: who else is around?

What: what action preceded the urge?[5]

When I was trying to get into a regular morning prayer and Bible-reading time, my problem was not so much that I was forgetting about it, but that I was having a hard time convincing myself to actually do it when the time came. I'm a morning person, so I picked first thing in the morning for the time I wanted to set aside. Only, my alarm came…and went. Over and over, it happened this way until I *had* to get up to go to work.

This was becoming my habit: set my alarm for way earlier than it needed to be (for work), it goes off, and for the next hour, dip in and out of consciousness as I hit snooze over and over.

This whole set-the-alarm-an-hour-early plan was failing with astonishing precision, and as a result, this last hour of sleep was not very productive. So I either had to stop doing this,[6] or make some other change so that I'd actually get up.

So I asked Duhigg's questions:

Where was I? In bed.

What time was it? *Too* early.

What was my emotional state? Asleep.

Who else was around? Just Kristin, my wife. But she was fast asleep (or trying to be).

And, What action preceded the urge?

The answer to that last one didn't come initially. I was asleep. *Nothing* preceded it. Then as I thought about it more, and it hit me: *sleep* was the action that preceded my urge to keep sleeping. Understanding this proved to be the key to eventually getting up.

Generally, I was getting enough sleep, but I was still having trouble waking up. So I started using Northcube's Sleep Cycle app. It monitors your sleep either by motion or sound (I use sound), and it wakes you up as much as 30 to 45 minutes *before* your alarm goes off. The reason for this is because it's monitoring your sleep cycles to wake you up at the best time, when your body is most *willing* to get up. After a few nights of using this app as my alarm, I was getting up and feeling great. Finally, I'd cracked my getting-up problem.

The power of these five questions is that they bring *awareness*. That's what led me to trying a new alarm, and to eventually get up on purpose.

Awareness is like an epiphany showing your eyes the truth for the first time. Absolutely nothing else in the world may have changed, but once you *know* certain things, *you've* changed. This is why many social movements focus their efforts on awareness. They believe that once people are presented with the truth in the right context, the motivation will follow.

"It seems ridiculously simple," says behavioral psychologist Nathan Azrin, "but once you're aware of how your habit works, once you recognize the cues and rewards, you're halfway to changing it."[7]

Awareness is what helped me fix my second problem, too.

You see, once I got up, I was having a hard time getting to my Bible reading. I'd play online, or do some writing, but I was squeezing out the purpose of getting up in the first place: to read my Bible.

Let me back up and tell you first about the coffee (it's not what you think).

I like coffee (a *lot*, actually), but I don't *need* coffee.

Caffeine, as far as I can tell, doesn't have any effect on waking me up, or keeping me up. I can drink coffee before falling asleep, and I can wake up in the morning and go on just fine without it.[8] (In fact, when I'm traveling, I sometimes skip it altogether for several days at a time, and I never get the normal caffeine headaches.)

But I still drink the stuff like mad.

So I made a decision. When I'm up early in the morning, while I'm drinking my first cup, I'll read my Bible and pray during that time. I made a rule that that first cup was part of my morning prayer routine.

By attaching coffee to my morning prayer time, coffee became my *second cue*. After I was up, I was motivated to make coffee. So I didn't have to set anything in motion there. My only decision was to tack it onto what I was already doing. This is called stacking (more on that in chapter three).

Awareness is our single greatest tool for finding our cues. Once we've isolated what's setting off a routine, it's just a matter of tweaking it to get a new habit started.

THE TIME WITH THE OREOS

So far, we've looked at finding cues to get *new* habits started.

But the problem doesn't always start here. While it's important that we get good things rolling in our lives, if we don't make *room* for them in our already too busy schedules, then we won't have anywhere to put them. So, how do we make room?

This is best explained with Oreos.

It's really more of a confession. I...*have an Oreo problem*. Like, on the scale of eating a *sleeve* of Oreos a day.

After I get home from work, I grab the Oreos before I've even hung up my keys. Mid to late afternoons are the worst for me. Especially after I've been in traffic. My blood sugar is low and my willpower is even lower.

I need a kick to make it through the rest of the day.

So I eat lots and *lots* of sugar.

And, I hate to say it, but it works. Ten minutes later, after having consumed a week's supply of Oreos, I feel better. I have energy.

Of course, that energy is all simple-carb sugar. Which means that I have to work pretty hard to keep from crashing in the next hour. But still, in the moment, it's a solution.

I knew this was bad for a lot of reasons. That much sugar, especially without exercise to burn it off, isn't good for my body. Plus it really doesn't help the rest of my day. The essence of my problem was that I needed a pick-me-up to recover from a long day and stop-and-go traffic.

So I started asking myself the five questions. I wanted to know what it was that was causing this. Did my body *need* to binge on sugar? Or was I doing that as an answer to another problem?

Where, when, how, who, and what? It was every weekday (not on the weekends), when I got home from work. I needed a pick-me-up, and I was often the first one home. What action preceded it? Thirty to 45 minutes of mind-numbing stop-and-go traffic.

And that was it. Before, I thought the problem was that I was tired, and so four pounds of sugar was the kick-start I needed to wake back up. But after I thought about these questions, I found that wasn't it at all. My *brain* was tired from sitting in traffic, and the sugar was, in a way, waking it back up. But really what I needed was *stimulation*.

In other words, sugar wasn't the only answer to my problem.

For me, I love to read. As Gretchen Ruben has written, books are both my playground and my cubical. I do a lot of research for my writing and work, but I also read for fun, and that's something that energizes me. So I decided to do an experiment. Before the kids get home, I'd read for 15-20 minutes immediately after I get out of brain cell-killing traffic. And it would be something I enjoy. No work. Just 100 percent feel-good stuff.

And just like that, I didn't need the Oreos.

At first, I'd eat peanuts or something salty, just to put something in my mouth. But because my body doesn't get high off of salt like it does sugar, salt helped curb the need-to-put-something-in-mouth part of the habit. And now my brain has something that wakes it back up (reading), which was what it *really* needed in the first place.

Let's put this into habit terminology. Traffic was my cue. Oreos were my routine (which I replaced with a few minutes of stimulating reading). And my awakened brain was my reward.

I mentioned before that rewards and cues work together. In order for you to make a change that *sticks*, you have to tap into something that you actually do want. I wanted stimulation and a quick snack. That turned into an epic Oreo binge. But by focusing on my cue and reward, I was able to fairly easily replace Oreos with reading and a few peanuts. So why did that work?

CUES ARE PINNED TO REWARDS

During the reward phase, the brain releases dopamine, which feels...*great*.

This happens when the routine makes good on the promise of the cue. If you're stressed out and then you light up, the nicotine from the cigarette relaxes your blood vessels making you feel less stressed. Your brain congratulates the rest of your body by releasing dopamine as a way of saying: *I liked that, do it again.* (Of course, smoking creates its own problems by *causing* those blood vessels to be constricted in the first place. So, not to turn in to a PSA, but really cigarettes are more like the mafia: they're saving you from the very problems they've created. Which is, incidentally, why cigarettes are such a powerful example to explain how rewards fuel the habit cycle.)

It doesn't take long for your brain to associate the reward directly with the cue. And once established, it's like a short-circuit, skipping the full justification and going straight for the good stuff. In Ivan Pavlov's famous example ("Pavlov's dog"), he fed his dogs every day immediately after ringing a dinner bell. Soon the dogs began to salivate as soon as they heard the bell—even before they'd seen the food. The dog's brain, and ours too, learns to anticipate rewards based on cues. This is the reward kicking in *before* the routine even happens (which is why the reward works so well).

This is also why missing a day or two in the process is not a cause for alarm. In the habit-forming study I cited at the beginning of this chapter, psychologist Jeremy Dean reports that "contrary to what's commonly believed, missing a day or two didn't much affect habit formation."[9] And I've experienced this myself. In fact, my weekends are often completely different from my weekdays, yet, come Monday, I'm right back into my normal routines.

Understanding this helps when we screw up—which in my case is more common than when I don't. My first reaction to missing a routine (like sleeping in) is to think I'm not making any progress or my technique is wrong or, fill in the blank—the obstacles are too great.

But truly, the victory goes to the one who perseveres. Like the study of the guy who was trying to create a morning habit of 50 sit-ups. Some things are hard. And they just take a while.

Speaking of hard, your routine might legitimately be a hard thing, but your cues never should be.

CUE TRIPPER[10]

When you're adding a new habit, like a daily prayer time, you'll be most successful if it's easy. And the easier it is, the more successful you'll be.

Right.

No surprise to any of us there (and, you're probably considering putting this book down now that you see what kind of mind-numbingly obvious advice you're getting).

But don't. Not yet. Stick with it, because this is one of the best ways to find good cues. When I'm looking for or creating new cues, if they don't pass this test, I don't even consider them.

Here it is: *You need to trip over your cue.*

It needs to be that obvious.

In *Making Habits, Breaking Habits,* Dean writes "that the best cue…is something that happens every day at a regular time."[11] This kind of predictability is a good way to trip over your cue. Something every day at the same time is just going to happen whether you remember it or not. And because that's true, you can latch on to it much more easily than if you're building something from the ground up.

I think of it like this: if I want to visit some place overseas like Paris, I'm going to need to fly there. So I can either build or buy my own plane, or I can get a ticket from a company that already does that sort of thing. I'm not into building planes. So I'm going to go the much easier route and buy a ticket on someone else's.

Habits are the same. If you want to be successful, you have to focus on making it as easy as possible. You need to trip over your cue.

SECRET SAUCE

Secret Sauce: Motivation

If you're not *motivated* to do something, none of this will work. It all hinges on you *wanting* to make the change. Life hacking is not about short-cuts, it's about smart-cuts: doing things that make sense.

So if you're trying to do something you're convinced won't work (and while you might need to keep up the pretense for your social circles) don't believe the stories yourself. Make it easy on yourself and move on to something you *want* to do.

But wanting something doesn't mean having all the answers, or even an air-tight plan. I've seen a lot of dumb small-business owners succeed because they wanted it. Sometimes being dumb is an asset because that keeps you from seeing all the ways you can fail.

The secret sauce in all of this is to *want it*. When you want something, you tend to find a way to make it happen. My purpose in this book is not to help you find the want, but to give you a leg up on the want you've already got.

FAILURE SAUCE

Creating habits, and remembering how all of this stuff works, tends to fly out of the window in the middle of temptation or trouble. Under stress is the last place you want to be trying something new.

So, I suggest: *don't.*

Don't wait until you need these changes in place to begin implementing them. Doing that is going to put you perpetually behind the curve. And playing catch-up on hard, new things usually fails. Making changes is always an uphill battle, so here are two practical strategies to help you mitigate failure and get ahead of the curve.

First, take some time now, when it's still quiet, to visualize how you're going to make these changes. How are you going to create a regular prayer and Bible reading time? What cues make the most sense to you? What are your triggers for lapsing into the habits that keep you from going in the direction you want?

Better yet, I suggest getting out paper (do you *have* paper? You probably have a printer...that has paper... somewhere. Or, you can flip to the back of this book). Get out something to write, then go into as much detail as you can. Write down exactly what you want to start doing (for instance, "reading my Bible for fifteen minutes each morning"), and then write down exactly where you're going to fail (like, "I always snooze my alarm, which puts me behind schedule and makes me late for work, and I don't have time to squeeze in an extra fifteen minutes"). And then write down how you're going to keep that problem from happening ("I'm going to pack my lunch the night before," or "iron my clothes the night before," or "just go to bed earlier"). The deeper you think through this now on paper, the more natural it will be when the time comes to implement it. You might change your plan when it comes time to do it (and that's okay), but thinking it through now begins feeding your subconscious, and it allows your brain to do what it does best.

I'll warn you: this step is hard. It's like digging a run-off ditch. Lots of manual labor and sweat there. But digging a ditch is still a whole lot easier than trying to control where rain water goes by running out there as its falling from the sky and trying to catch it with your hands.[12]

The second strategy is to be okay with failing. Your *goal* isn't to fail. And staying motivated really is key. But if you assume the burden of your failure, then you're not going to last to the end. When we put ourselves under a microscope, we see that we fail a lot more than we might like to think. And, that's okay. That's part of it. Instead, you need to be able to live in a state of forgiveness with yourself.

If you're like me (and I'm learning a lot of people are like this), you keep a mental scorecard for yourself. The scorecard grades you on how much you get wrong—a lot like school. But that sort of thinking has a fundamental hole in it. It's the opposite of grace. If we continue to think of ourselves like this, we'll never be able to live in forgiveness. And, much more importantly, we'll never be able to live the liberated life that we've been given as a follower of Jesus.

This mental shift is important. But, that doesn't mean we should get rid of the scorecard. I don't think living with *no* standard is the answer. Instead, we should change how the score card works. What I mean is, all of our goals stay in place, but how we *measure* those goals is what we begin to change.

Instead of defining winning by how much we get right, we need to define winning by how long we've been playing. In other words, the game is not about doing it perfect (getting a 100 on the test), but is instead about endurance—not quitting.

The reason this shift is so effective is that we're all constantly messing up. And after a while, we see all that and it's hard to believe we still even belong in the game. But we do. We definitely do.

And so by changing the way we grade ourselves—by asking these new questions: "Am I still in the game?" And, "Am I still giving this my full effort?"—we will find it much easier to find motivation. And it's also here that we'll be able to live in the forgiveness and grace our Lord has already given us. When what we first tried didn't work, we'll be able to honestly know that it's okay. We're not failures. Instead, we'll keep trying and honing, because eventually, we know that through perseverance it *will* work.

NOTES

[1] Strange, Elmira, *Lose Weight in 21 Days:: Stress- and Weight Loss Program for Busy Women* (Amazon Digital Services LLC, 2016).

[2] Lapointe, Lauren, *21 Days to Creativity: How to Develop a Creative Practice* (International Creative, 2016).

[3] Sisson, Mark, *Transformation: A step-by-step, gene reprogramming action plan* (Primal Nutrition, Inc., 2011).

[4] Dean, Jeremy, *Making Habits, Breaking Habits* (Da Capo Press, 2013) 5-6.

[5] http://charlesduhigg.com/how-habits-work/ accessed July 5th, 2016.

[6] "and stop waking up my wife," says my wife.

[7] http://psychcentral.com/blog/archives/2012/07/17/the-golden-rule-of-habit-change/, accessed July 23, 2016.

[8] What I mean here is that coffee doesn't energize me enough to make a difference in the way I feel; however, for most people, drinking coffee before bed is not a good idea. Even if you're like me, studies show that caffeine still has an effect on your sleep, and it's good to hold off at least six hours before you go to bed. http://www.aasmnet.org/jcsm/ViewAbstract.aspx?pid=29198, accessed July 24, 2016.

[9] Dean, Jeremy, *Making Habits, Breaking Habits* (Da Capo Press, 2013) 5.

[10] I completely stole this from the Beatles' song, "Day Tripper." Beyond this vague reference, they don't have much to do with each other.

[11] Dean, Jeremy *Making Habits, Breaking Habits* (Da Capo Press, 2013) 141.

[12] The point of this absurd illustration is that it's *impossible* to catch the rain with our hands. But the ditch—while hard to dig—makes it possible.

chapter three

WILLPOWER WON'T POWER

"I am, indeed, a king, because I know how to rule myself."
- Pietro Aretino

There's a reoccurring theme in the *Lethal Weapon* movie series. Roger (Danny Glover) finds himself in a predicament and always says the same thing: "I'm getting too old for this."

And that's usually contrasted by his younger, and at times hyperactive, partner Riggs (Mel Gibson), who's typically getting them into more shenanigans. In the fourth movie, the series is feeling the weight of the actors' real ages. In one scene, Gibson's character, Riggs, finally admits that he too might be "getting too old for this."

But then he stops himself mid-thought.

"I won't accept it," he says. "I'll *will it* not to happen."

In the scene, they were working up the courage to stop a guy with a massive flame thrower wearing head-to-toe body armor. And their solution? They're going to *will* themselves to be able to handle it.

That's kind of funny.

It also highlights an important assumption about our willpower. The way we look at things *does* make a difference. But the stuff itself—willpower—seems to be surrounded more by legend than fact. As health psychologist Kelly McGonigal has observed, "much of what people believed about willpower was sabotaging their success and creating unnecessary stress."[1]

Her research dispels the myth that some people—successful people—simply have an abundance of willpower. Rather, "one thing the science of willpower makes clear," she writes, "is that everyone struggles in some way with temptation, addiction, distraction, and procrastination."[2]

Yet, what is it that allows some of us to make a way forward, while the rest of us are perpetually stuck at the starting line?

McGonigal gives three bits of advice on how to leverage your willpower the way it's meant to be used.

FIRST, I WANT IT

Start with what you want most, what she calls your "I want" power.[3] In essence, this is a matter of sitting down and determining what's most important. If you're trying to get into a prayer habit, but you're wanting to sleep in, it's important to remember *why* you're trying to get into this new habit. This is the same idea that compels successful athletes to, "recognize that the first wave of fatigue is never a real limit"[4] We have to mentally prioritize so that we have the motivation to push through when it gets hard.

SECOND, I FLEX IT

Begin thinking about your willpower like a muscle. Much of our willpower failure is like trying to run a marathon without even having gone for a jog. We're completely out of shape. It's not that we *can't* run the marathon, it's that we just aren't in shape yet. "When you're trying to make a big change," writes McGonigal, "look for a small way to practice self-control that strengthens your willpower; but doesn't overwhelm it completely."[5] For me, when I'm trying to get back into a morning routine I've fallen out of, I'll move my alarm clock up by 15 minutes, and leave it there for a few days, sometimes as long as a week. Some people recommend doing 10 minutes every day, but I don't find this works. That's too much. For me, it's a much longer process.

THIRD, I FORGIVE IT

This is by far the most fascinating of her advice: incorporate forgiveness. A Carleton University study tracking student procrastination found that "forgiveness—not guilt—helped them get back on track."[6] What is interesting to me is that their conclusion is the same core message of the Gospel: success is based on forgiveness. Many times we're driven by something to make a change. We want to help others, or we know that we need to get ourselves into a different place. Whatever the case is, the path of change is littered with setbacks and failures. To be extraordinarily cliché, Edison's quote about succeeding in the face of 10,000 failures comes to mind.[7] He instead reframes the issue: they weren't failures, they were just road markers. Sometimes those road markers can be extremely frustrating. So frustrating they make us question why we're trying at all. If we continually double-down on our poor willpower, we probably won't make it.

Willpower can be used for great things, but it's a process. Those who are most successful understand best—often by trial and error—how to use willpower the way it was *intended*.

THE PROGRESS OF AUTOPILOT

When psychologist Roy Baumeister, an industry leader in willpower, teamed up with *New York Times* science writer John Tierney, their goal was to advance the understanding of willpower mechanics. "Most major problems, personal and social," they write in *Willpower,* "center on a failure of self-control."[8] In a study attempting to predict students' success rates, "self-control turned out to be the *only* trait that predicted a college student's grade-point average better than chance." Noting that while "raw intelligence was obviously an advantage, the study showed that self-control was more important."[9]

This is intriguing because it puts the outcome of our success back in our own laps. It's not so much who we are but *what* we do that matters.

This idea was pushed to the extreme many years before this kind of research was being measured in the often hard to read accounts of the famous nineteenth-century journalist and explorer Henry Stanley.

Stanley and his men explored the interior of Africa, and, as their journals attest, death was common, starvation was normal, and sanity seemed to come and go. When you wake up without food and with a stomach severely out of line from disease and parasite, what's first on the morning's roster, asks Baumeister? "For Stanley," after perhaps a quick callback to nature, "this was an easy decision: shave."[10]

His men, most of whom died or deserted, were slowly starving to death, and hope was perhaps what was endangered most. Yet Henry Stanley still makes the pained effort, even with a dull blade, to shave every morning. Why? As Stanley biographer Tim Jeal explains, "the creation of order can only have been an antidote to the destructive capacities of nature all around him."[11] Stanley had control of very little in such a wild place. But the control he did have allowed him to tap into a kind of autopilot, and "once he had expended the willpower to *make* it his custom, it became a relatively automatic mental process requiring little or no further willpower."[12]

This kind of thinking is the key to self-control. Because "orderly habits like that can actually *improve* self-control in the long run by triggering automatic mental processes that don't require much energy."[13] In like vein, Baumeister's research went on to find that "people with high self-control were distinguished by their behaviors that took place more or less automatically."[14]

In other words, smarts help, but self-control is often the determiner of success. And that same self-control is best created and preserved in the form of a habit.

There's a famous quote by Martin Luther. I wish it were really his. People cite him for it all the time, but as far as I can find, we don't have any record of where he actually said it (though scholars have said it sounds like something he could very well have said). The quote is this: "I have so much to do that I shall spend the first three hours in prayer."

I hope it's genuine, because it's true. The only way you can get to three hours of prayer in the face of a threateningly busy schedule is to have first, once upon a time, started with five minutes. Which then at some point grew to 15. And so on. It's the habit formation that allows such feats to be possible. Like every kind of training, you do it day in and day out so that when the real challenge is presented, you are ready.

This is what willpower does for you. It gets you started on the small stuff, so that habit can take over and graduate you to the big stuff.

STACKING

Stacking builds on the momentum you've already got rolling. I referenced this in chapter two. In essence, it's when you put one habit behind another already established habit.

Most of the time when we're excited to start something new, we put it in a vacuum void of reality. If I heard a great speaker, who talked about his prayer time, which made me excited to get up early and fire back up my quiet time, I'll just set my alarm early. Problem solved. Life is good. God's great. Praise the Lord!

And that works for about as long as it took to read that last paragraph. Eventually, usually sooner than later, reality sets in. I can't get myself to work on time on a normal day; how am I going to *add* something to my morning schedule? Or, once the kids wake up, our house is pure and unadulterated chaos, and I'm supposed to, what, learn to pause all that while I sit quietly to pray?

Not exactly.

Behavioral scientist BJ Fogg explains that stacking requires three things: motivation, ability, and a cue[15]. There are two important parts when picking a stacking cue. The first is to pin it to something you already do. That might be as simple as getting out of bed every morning, or putting on your shirt after you get out of the shower, or brushing your teeth before bed. Whatever it is, use this well established habit as your anchor. This anchor will be the cue for your new habit.

The next thing Fogg recommends is to start with what he calls a "tiny habit." In his 2012 TEDxFremont talk, he highlights the extreme example of only flossing one tooth a day. He stacked this onto his current habit of brushing his teeth, and then only attempted to floss *one* tooth a day.[16]

When I shared my morning routine earlier, and how I set the time immediately after pouring my first cup of coffee as my Bible reading time, that was an example of stacking. I used something that wasn't in question (as all *true* coffee drinkers know), and like jumping onto a moving train, I tacked onto it my new habit: morning Bible reading.

James Clear, who makes his living teaching others how to develop habits, explains that this is because of "synaptic pruning." From the time we're born until now, our brains are constantly pruning out connections that we don't need. What to keep and what to prune out is determined by how often we use it. "The more you do something," writes Clear, "the stronger and more efficient the connection becomes."[17] And the rest, things like chatter in a crowd or TV commercials, get classified as junk and deleted.

Synoptic pruning is why tiny habits work. By doing something over and over, your brain learns that this action is relevant to your life (because it keeps showing up), and so the neural path gets strengthened instead of deleted. Tiny habits also work because they're so ridiculously small, it would take more energy to talk yourself out of them than to just get them over with. Like flossing one tooth. You *want* to get into a flossing habit. But what excuse can you reasonably think of that would be easier than just flossing one tooth?

Before I sat down to write this book, I interviewed a lot of people. Of everyone who was a self-professed Christian, I asked the question: how's your prayer life?

With almost 100 percent consistency, I heard the same thing over and again: *it could be better.*

When I pressed for more specifics, the majority said they struggled with making it regular. They wanted to pray every day, but were inconsistent. Or they wanted to pray for a long time, but kept getting distracted.

Concepts like stacking and tiny habits help tremendously in establishing a regular and consistent prayer time.

If you want to get into a habit of reading your Bible every day before you leave for work or school, then find something you know you'll do every morning. If it's eating breakfast, then put a sticky note next to your cereal bowls, so that when you grab a bowl, you remember to grab your Bible, too. That's the stacking part. You won't be burdening yourself with remembering.

But the second step is equally important. You need to start small. As in, just a *few* minutes a day.

Most days you'll easily be able to do more, but some days you won't. What you want your brain to do is to get used to reading your Bible every morning. How much you read is not important right now—only *that* you read. Once you're beginning to establish these neural highways that include a regular and consistent Bible reading time, you'll find yourself getting into the shower a few minutes earlier, or doing the ironing the night before, so that you can squeeze in a few more minutes.

A hurried few minutes is not the end result. But it is the starter.

PEOPLE KNOW ME

In his book *Contagious* Jonah Berger looks at why things catch on. In the 80s and 90s Nancy Reagan's "Just Say No" campaign was wildly popular. It was so popular that about a decade later Congress apportioned another $1 billion toward a similar anti-drug campaign.[18]

But did it work? Did drug use among kids actually decline?

One of Berger's premises in his book is that *visible* things catch on much faster than non-visible things. This is due to "Behavioral Residue," a term coined by psychologist Sam Gosling.[19] This is when products sell themselves because their use is public and creates its own advertising. Social media sites, like Facebook, have high behavioral residue. What your friends do shows up in your news feed. And by virtue of their posts and likes, you can watch them using the product, and Facebook doesn't have to do any advertising. Then if you like what you see, you'll be inclined to keep looking or join in.

And ironically, this is why the "Just Say No" campaigns failed. According to a study by Bob Hornik of the University of Pennsylvania, drug use among kids actually *increased* during these campaigns.[20] As Berger notes, this is because the campaigns made drug use *more* visible.

Berger explains:

> Imagine you're a fifteen-year-old who has never considered using drugs. You're sitting at home watching cartoons one afternoon when a public service announcement comes on telling you about the dangers of drug use. Someone's going to ask you if you want to try drugs and you need to be ready to say no. Or even worse, the cool kids are going to be the ones asking. But you shouldn't say yes.[21]

The drug campaigns were relying on willpower. But willpower alone wasn't enough. And because it was a campaign of awareness, it highlighted the strength of its greatest enemy: peer pressure.

Willpower has its place, but putting too great a burden on it will often result in failure. Willpower functions like the match that starts the fire, not the campfire itself. If you don't have something for the match to set fire *to*, you won't have much of a campfire.

Every Tuesday I meet with my friend, Daylon. We talk about life and what's bothering us and what's going well. And then we pray for each other. The more I share with Daylon, the more accountable I am to him. And the same for him to me.

This kind of personal visibility goes a long way to staying on the straight and narrow. I can maintain a public persona fairly well. I'm not super-active on social media, and I'm not too reactive on what I post. But on a one-on-one basis, talking with someone I respect and trust, who I am is what comes out.

The truth is, in our individualized culture, positive and supportive relationships are one of the most important things we can do for our spiritual growth. When we put ourselves around people who don't value these things, we take upon ourselves the entire burden of keeping going day after day. Even though I might not talk to Daylon for six out of seven days, that regular Tuesday is enough to reinforce that I have someone who wants to know how I'm doing.

These kinds of relationships shift the emphasis from our own willpower to, instead, making the practice of spiritual disciplines a behavioral residue, which is to say, something we are attracted to.

And while these relationships are important for development, they become critical for survival.

POSITIONING

I'm the kind of person that lets the gas tank in my car get to E. And then, I drive it around a few more days with that little shining amber light staring up at me before I refill.

I'm not really sure why I do this.

When I was in college my truck actually died on me because I ran out of gas. I had just enough momentum to coast into a gas station (true story). A few months ago, my wife and I took the kids to Tennessee to visit her parents, and we almost had another coast-into-gas-station moment. You'd think after these years I'd have learned.

Warning signs, like that little *you're out of gas* light, are good…if we pay attention to them.

And fortunately, once we learn to pay attention, our willpower has warning signs, too.

Baumeister in his willpower research has found that it's often not a single sign to look out for, "but rather for a change in the *overall intensity* of your feelings."[22] In a 2005 study published in the *Journal of Social and Clinical Psychology*, researchers watched college students before exam time and noticed significant behavioral changes. They stopped exercising and consumed about twice as much caffeine. Which is really a surprise to no one, because exam time is cram time.

But that's not where the study ended. Apparently, the student's cigarette and alcohol consumption went up markedly, and—no surprise—many students reported their study habits worsened during exam time. What researchers found was that "what stress really does, though, is deplete willpower, which diminishes your ability to control" yourself.[23]

If we know in advance where we are going to fail, like times when stress is high, we can prepare ourselves by where we go and what we put in our paths. What this teaches us is that our natural instinct is to rely more heavily on willpower than we should, which often produces the exact opposite effect—a willpower crash.

So how do we handle these intense and stressful times? In an article on Psychology Today's website, James Clear gives a big dose of credit to our environment. "When your willpower is depleted," writes Clear, "you are even more likely to make decisions based on the environment around you."[24] But if you are intentional about your environment, intentionally putting good things in reach and bad things out of sight—what he calls "choice architecture"—then you will "automatically do the right thing without worrying about willpower or motivation. If you design your environment to make the default choice a better one, then it's more likely that you'll make a good choice now and have more willpower leftover for later."[25]

By taking a few proactive steps to move things that you know will distract you, and replace them with things you know you need, you'll find much of the battle has already been won.

I do this by leaving my Bible on the floor of my office in my house. I don't do my prayer time sitting at my desk, because that's where I do all my other work. Instead, I do my prayer time on the floor next to one of my bookshelves, sitting on a pillow (that my wife tells me actually belongs on our couch). And so I leave my Bible right there on the floor. Each morning when I wake up, I have to choose to *ignore* it, rather than choosing to get it out. That little bit of positioning gives me a willpower advantage. Instead of needing willpower to do what I *want* to do, I now have to use willpower to *not* do what I want. Which means I end up doing what I want. Only now with less effort and a higher success rate.

All these years later and the words of Oscar Wilde are still ringing true: I can resist *everything*...except temptation.

And as long as the temptations are good, who cares?

That's what positioning is about.

NOTES

[1] McGonigal, Kelly, *The Willpower Instinct* (Penguin Group, 2012), 2.

[2] Ibid., 5.

[3] Ibid., 10.

[4] Ibid., 72.

[5] Ibid., 69.

[6] Ibid., 148.

[7] In case you're not familiar, what he said was: "I have not failed. I've just found 10,000 ways that won't work."

[8] Baumeister, Roy F., John Tierney, *Willpower* (Penguin Press, 2011), 2.

[9] Ibid., 11-12.

[10] Ibid., 155.

[11] Ibid., 156.

[12] Ibid., 157. Emphasis mine.

[13] Ibid., 156. Emphasis mine.

[14] Ibid., 157.

[15] His verbiage is "trigger," but it's the same thing, so for consistency I'm calling it a cue.

[16] https://www.youtube.com/watch?v=AdKUJxjn-R8, accessed July 81, 2016.

[17] http://jamesclear.com/habit-stacking, accessed July 18, 2016.

[18] Berger, Jonah, *Contagious: Why Things Catch On* (Simon & Schuster, 2013), 150.

[19] Gosling, Sam, *Snoop: What Your Stuff Says About You* (Basic Books, 2009), 28.

[20] Hornik, Robert, Lela Jacobsohn, Robert Orwin, Andrea Piesse, and Graham Kalton (2008), "Effects of the National Youth Anti-Drug Media Campaign on Youths," *American Journal of Public Health* 98, no. 12, 2229-36.

[21] Berger, Jonah, *Contagious: Why Things Catch On* (Simon & Schuster, 2013), 151.

[22] Baumeister, Roy F., John Tierney, *Willpower* (Penguin Press, 2011), 30. Emphasis mine.

[23] Ibid., 33.

[24] https://www.psychologytoday.com/blog/slow-gains/201403/how-stick-good-habits-when-your-willpower-is-gone, accessed July 25, 2016.

[25] https://www.psychologytoday.com/blog/slow-gains/201403/how-stick-good-habits-when-your-willpower-is-gone, accessed July 25, 2016.

chapter four
THE ART OF FOCUSING

"Tell me to what you pay attention and I will tell you who you are."
- José Ortega y Gasset

Attention works much like a muscle," writes psychologist Daniel Goleman, "use it poorly and it can wither; work it well and it grows."[1]

Goleman is most known for his work in Emotional Intelligence, which measures a person's self-awareness as well as how they relate to others. For decades he has researched behavioral success. One idea that's been prominent is that focus is not a thing some have and others don't, it's more a thing some *cultivate* and other don't. "Smart practice," says Goleman, "can further develop and refine the muscle of our attention, even rehab [sic] focus-starved brains."[2]

For a lot of us, Goleman's conclusions are a double -edged sword. On the one hand, it means we're not permanently stuck in our reactive smartphone-addicted states.

But on the other hand, it means that the ball's been left in our court—we are the ones responsible for making changes happen.

For me in particular, I too often find myself glued to the dings and little red dots that show up on my iPhone. Chick-fil-a has clearly seen a trend of a lot of people doing this, because they've started giving away free ice-cream for anyone who can go the entire meal without checking their device.[3]

(Speaking of life hacks—as is the point of this book—I've mostly solved my phone-addiction just by turning off the notifications for 95% of my apps.[4] Turning these little guys off is another example of positioning from the last chapter.)

And while removing distractions goes a long way toward focusing, the act itself requires a bit more. Unless we intentionally replace those distractions with something else, the chaos will return. It's for this concept that I'm defining focus as an *active movement* in an *specific direction*.

In other words, it involves you making a decision about what you want, and then taking steps in that direction.

In many ways, focus is what reveals our true identities —it allows what's truly important to have center stage. But with that comes a kind of discipline. As Henry Cloud writes, "it is extremely important to be able to make negative assertions. We must be able to say what is 'not me' in order to have a 'me'."[5]

When I was in high school, I had the hardest time studying. If I was alone, I was unaccountable and my mind drifted. If I was in public, I would wonder what others were working on and couldn't stick to my own stuff. When my atmosphere was noisy, the sounds were too much. And when everything was quiet, I would listen until I could *find* sounds, and then I couldn't focus because, well, there were sounds.

Then, one day, years later, everything changed.

As if overnight, I could tune it all out, and focusing wasn't a problem anymore. So what happened?

My interests aligned with my studies. This, says Goleman, is an important ingredient in what he calls *flow*. "When you get up in the morning, are you happy about getting to work, school, or whatever it is that occupies your day?"[6] Because, he continues, if you're not, you're not likely to get into the flow necessary to focus.[7] It's your *interest* that carries the leverage of your focus.

The issue of the gap is: I am here, but I want to be there. What gets me across? Here are two starters I use most mornings.

First, in the spiritual disciplines, all roads lead from praise. Praise is a kind of spiritual recalibrator. The Psalms are replete with how worship and praise are integral to not only our health, but our very existence.[8] Praise is the single greatest readjustment we have at our constant and ready disposal.

Part of the power of praise is that it allows us to see ourselves more for who we are, and to see God more for who He is. When we get to that point, while our problems and distractions all still exist, they exist in the context of a stronger God. The Creator. And the One who loves us on a level we cannot fully compute.

Second is writing. I don't mean *writing,* like writing a book. I mean only the effort of moving your thoughts from your head to your hand.[9] This exercise forces you to solidify otherwise soft thoughts. And it has a way of bringing your mind into focus.

I keep a notebook next to my Bible, and sometimes I'll start by writing whatever is on my mind, like if something significant happened yesterday. Other times, I might go a week or more without writing anything. I don't keep to any "dear diary" form. I just write. And it's something I only do for me. That takes a lot of the pressure off. When I'm feeling connected and ready, I immediately switch over and begin praying. This is not so much a time for structure as it is for getting started.

The rest of this chapter looks at ways to increase focus specifically for spiritual disciplines.

BREATHE IN...

The idea of spiritual disciplines can be intimidating: things like fasting and hours of prayer. But these are *results*. These are things that come later. A friend of mine, Rich, is now retired. He's told me about his morning prayer routine that often goes for well over an hour. "Sometimes, an hour isn't enough," said Rich, "and I just need more time."

More time? *For what?*

But that's the thing. The more you learn to spend time with God, the more you depend on and desire that time. In part, this is the neural wiring I talked about earlier. It's your brain both repeating what it does often (neural pathways), but also craving the good reward (the habit cycle). And while those things are certainly helpful to the process, there's something else going on.

I am writing this in the summer of 2016. It started, in Orlando, with the largest mass shooting in U.S. history. Then a black man was shot by police in Baton Rouge. Following this, another black man in Minnesota. Then a police ambush in Dallas, killing five. Followed by a different ambush on police in Baton Rouge, less than a week later, this time killing three more officers.

Two weeks ago a man in a truck drove through a crowd in Nice, France, killing *eighty*, and just yesterday in Normandy a 19-year-old boy cuts off an elderly priest's head, in the name of ISIS.

It's been a rough and sad summer.

As soon as Orlando happened, many anti-gun lobbyists ramped up their efforts for tighter gun control. Alton Sterling's death in Baton Rouge kicked off a firestorm of protests, both for and against the police.

Regardless of where you come down on these issues, it's undeniable that these are *moral* problems. Yet, a freedom from the kind of objective morality these movements stand on is exactly what we see being lobbied for.[10]

The truth is, you don't have to be a Christian, or even an *anything* to know it's wrong for a man to open fire on an unarmed and innocent crowd, or for a man to drive a bus through a peaceful crowd of families.

In his book *Mere Christianity*[11], C.S. Lewis argues that the wrong the world is expressing over these events is the same objective morality God has placed in us all—the "image of God"[12] that we were all created with.

In wave after wave of violence, many have screamed out for answers. Where *is* God in the middle of this?

The answer is that God is where He's always been. Nothing escapes His attention, no wrong will go unpunished, and all will be put right in His time. But that doesn't mean God's passive. Far from it. He's active and moving. We live in the world created by *our* sin. Second Peter 3:9 says that it is for this very reason that God is *patient* in setting this all right—for as soon as He does, there will be no more chances. Whatever horror exists in this life, it is incomparable to an eternity being separated from Him.

Some days, when I'm stuck in my small world with its small problems, these thoughts are far from my consciousness. And if I'm not careful, I can fall into a lopsided view of it all—seeing the venom without remembering the antidote.

Reconnecting this deep and fundamental relationship —the spiritual journey—is done with a regular time in God's Word. It is here that we are reminded of the big picture.

So we breathe in. We take a moment to find quiet. And we immerse ourselves in the anchor of God.

Focusing always begins top-down. Remembering why what you're doing is important. From this place, the rest flows.

...AND OUT

Just like there needs to be a taking in, there must also be a letting out.

U.S. Census data has shown a regular decade over decade increase of people earning college and graduate degrees.[13] As a people, education is clearly important to us. In fact, there has been a counter-cultural resurgence, largely led by former *Dirty Jobs* host Mike Rowe, emphasizing the value of trade jobs.

In some ways it seems we're polarizing ourselves. One side is gaining more and more classroom experience, while the other side is focusing on old-fashioned hands-dirty work.

Both are necessary, but I suggest—somewhat anecdotally—that the best option is a blend of the two. After I graduated from college, I worked full time for six years before returning to graduate school. And while I was in graduate school, I continued to work full time. During that time I became a manager and had three people under me. That shouldn't mean anything to you other than to say I have seen the value of combining practical real world experience with theoretical mind-broadening education. The two shouldn't be in a battle but on a team.

Interestingly, our spiritual lives have a dynamic similar to this. Reading God's Word is good. But it's not enough. Doing *only* that leaves us lopsided. What balances us then?

Prayer.

Prayer turns the monolog into a dialog. Because of sin, we are fundamentally separated from God. The relationship we had was damaged. And as a result, we no longer have that open flow of communication. We all live seeking and knowing there is something better, but life keeps it obscured.

Prayer is the element God has given us to reconnect with him directly. Jesus told the story of the man who had lived a life against God, but then one day realized his error and cried humbly to God. He contrasted this man with another man, one who appeared to be living for God, but on the inside was only living for himself. Jesus said, putting all appearances aside, God was pleased with the first, not the second.

There's no right or wrong way to pray as long as it's honest. Prayer is about talking to God. If your intent is to do that, then you are succeeding.

These two elements—taking in God's Word and praying your heart back to Him—are the foundations of the spiritual disciplines. It's from here that everything else blossoms.

When you're starting out, getting to this point is like reaching your first plateau. You've climbed a great mountain and now you can finally rest in a place for a while. This is a good place to be.

But this isn't where it ends. No, the journey is much longer, and the rewards to come are still much sweeter.

The following tactics represent the three components of learning. They are deep, wide, and forward. Tactic 1 shows you how to puncture the superficial. Tactic 2 is about broadening that vein—branching out gives you perspective. And Tactic 3 is the key to making it stick.

TACTIC 1:
MEDITATING (OR, THINKING DEEP)

Meditation is the act of focusing. That's it.

Eastern and New Age beliefs have hijacked the term to have religious connotations. But in its purest form, it's a physical technique that allows you to calm your mind and body and to focus.

For me, meditation has become a critical factor for honing in and focusing, especially if I only have a short time.

Health Psychologist Kelly McGonigal writes, "that when you ask the brain to meditate, it gets better not just at meditating, but at a wide range of self-control skills, including attention, focus, stress management, impulse control, and self-awareness."[14] What is perhaps most interesting is the amount of time it takes to see progress happen. "One study found that just three hours of meditation practice led to improved attention and self-control. After eleven hours, researchers could see those changes in the brain."[15]

Other than the Eastern religious connotations, meditation tends to be thought of as something hard or long. But I've incorporated it into most of my morning prayer times, and the way I do it is neither hard nor long. I keep it easy and quick. In fact, I usually do it for only a minute or less. But that minute goes a long way.

In my meditation, I do a single breathing exercise.

When I first sit down to read and pray, if my mind is a buzz, or even just not yet awake, I'll sit comfortable but alert—usually in the lotus position. And everything else is slow and exaggerated. I breathe deeper than I normally do, I hold it for about a second, and then I slowly exhale.

I do this nine times, assigning one number to each in and out.

When I'm exhaling, I'm imagining my breath as smoke, filling and bouncing around the number I'm on. I imagine what the smoke looks like as it goes around the curves of the eight, or hits the corners of the four.

For me, I only ever need to go to nine. By that point, I'm relaxed and ready to move on. Most mornings this quick technique is a primer I use to get myself in the calm and focused frame of mind to begin my reading and prayer time.

TACTIC 2:
STUDYING (OR, GOING WIDE)

There's an old saying: "keep an open mind, but not so open that your brain falls out."

The idea is that there's a point when studying becomes bad. At some point, you can find yourself lost. And of course, the advice goes: be safe and stay away.

But I don't believe this is right. If you're grounded in truth, then exploration won't hurt. In fact, it usually helps. I remember the first time I read a book attacking the historical elements of the New Testament. It made me uncomfortable. *What if these claims are true?*

And that discomfort drove me to find the answers. (I've since come to learn that the New Testament collection is one of the best preserved and scholarly critical works from that time.[16] And with that my confidence has risen massively. But I wouldn't come anywhere near that conclusion if I hadn't first explored.)

For some, studying is a necessary evil from long ago. *Wasn't fun then—definitely don't want to bring it back now.*

And studying probably *is* a bad word for what I mean. Instead, I'm talking more about *exploring*. It can be free-form, or with the guide of a commentary or book. If you're like me, you do a little better on your own. Having someone tell you what to read next is more annoying than helpful. Or if you're like my wife, she prefers a guide. The right way is the way that helps you the most.

And that brings me to the only two qualifications of true studying. It should always be enlightening and interesting. That's it. But these two components are mission-critical. Everything else you can take it or leave it.

If it's not enlightening, then you're not actually learning, you're probably just torturing yourself. Okay, maybe that's too dramatic. But still, if you're not getting anything out of it, it's a waste of time. And who wants to waste time?

And if it's not interesting, then *why* are you doing it at all? In school, we had to learn lots of things that weren't interesting…like algebra. But now that you're an adult and past all that,[17] you're are already *in* life. And learning should have direct relevance to your life—be it for your job, a side interest, or—perhaps the most important of all—for your spiritual development.

As I mentioned a couple of sections back, studying is about broadening your perspective. To some, studying may seem like a peripheral issue or a luxury, but not a requirement. But this is a mistake. Studying is quite important to a healthy spiritual life. As Richard Foster in his foundational book *Celebration of Discipline* writes:

> Study is a specific kind of experience in which through careful attention to reality the mind is enabled to move in a certain direction. Remember, the mind will always take on an order conforming to the order upon which it concentrates.[18]

The mind will always take on an order conforming to the order upon which it concentrates. That's a cumbersome sentence, but it's key. What he's saying is, *you are what you eat.* If you're always putting lightweight stuff in, then you're only ever going to produce lightweight stuff.

Challenging books are the barbells in your gym. And studying is how you exercise the muscles of your brain.

TACTIC 3:
LEARNING (OR, MOVING FORWARD)

Kids are great learners because they immediately put into practice everything they see.

Hadley, my one-year-old, learns physics by pushing her juice cup off her tray and onto the floor. Over, and over, and over. Graham, my three-year-old, learns his numbers by counting everything. *Everything.* But this is how they learn. They see something and they immediately want to apply it.

Tactic 1 (meditation and focus) is about going deep. Tactic 2 (studying) is about exploring and widening your boundaries. Tactic 3 is all about application, and it builds on both tactics before it. If you're not *doing* anything with the knowledge you're accumulating, then you're not really learning. There's a theoretical kind of learning, but it lacks the real-world grounding that experience brings.

This is how it works. You spend time in God's Word, and soon He will begin to put things on your heart. They might come in the form of pain, or desire. But you will begin to feel a burden to do something. And unless you act on that, you will find your spiritual life begins to wane.

After more than three decades of ministry, Rick Warren is a man full of practical advice. I recall once hearing him address the issue of a church member complaining. He said, "often when someone criticizes you they are revealing their gifting and passions."

Of course, this is not always the case. But a good number of times, the person is being critical because they've stumbled onto a passion of their own, and they see it not being handled to their standard. Warren finished with the quip: "—and you might ought to hire them." His point was that when a person is passionate about something, they will put a high priority on getting it done right.

A few years back, I was in a similar situation, only *I* was that church member. In my church, I felt a lack of emphasis on apologetics—the discipline of defending the faith. Because I was on good terms with the staff, I proposed an idea: what if we had a class that could train regular attenders who are interested in practical ways to defend their faith?

They liked the idea and soon I was teaching *Questions and Faith*. Interestingly, during that time, I *learned* far more than I taught.

My point is this: learn to see the lack you observe, not as a criticism of the leadership, but as a prompting from God—maybe this is what He's putting on your heart to do. The church is a body, and everyone has their part.

Tactics 1 and 2 get you deep and wide. You can think of these as 2D. (Or, the X and Y axis from geometry.) But to get anywhere—in order to turn this model into a real-life 3D one, you need to add another component. And that's what this third tactic is all about.

You truly won't *learn* until you put in to practice what God is showing you.

This is a rocky path. But it's always that way. When you begin to do the *right* thing, there is pushback. Loads of it. And so here are two caveats, or warnings, to keep you on the straight and narrow.

CAVEAT, PART 1: SLOW & EASY

All successful ventures share one of the same principles: they pace themselves.

Speed is relative. You might be the one others are trying to keep up with, or you might be the one lagging a bit. Chances are, in most cases, there's a bit of both going on. You're going to find people ahead of you, and if you look, you'll be ahead of others.

My wife and I both love to read. On our honeymoon, we flew to Puerto Rico, which isn't a long flight from the southern side of the U.S. I was reading Bill Bryson's *In A Sunburned Country* and she was reading Katheryn Stockett's *The Help*—both full-sized books. The plane landed and she was almost done with her book. I was on chapter two of mine. I'm a slow reader.

But here's the thing. It really doesn't matter.

If I'm reading for entertainment, or retention, or enlightenment—whatever, I have to do it at the rate that is best for my brain.

Our spiritual lives are the same way. If you're gung-ho, great. But think about the long game. If you're going to start reading your Bible every morning, great. But make sure you're not setting yourself up to fail by putting aside too much time at first. Work up to that. God won't be mad. In fact, I think he appreciates when we think smart about these things.

When I was in school getting my master's degree, I was working full time, had a one-year-old at home, and my wife was pregnant with our second baby. I didn't realize it at the time—though writing it out now, it seems a bit obvious—but I was teetering at my limit.

Toward the end of my degree, in an effort to finish up, I took on too much and began to burn out. At first, I kept up. But it was rough. About three months into that schedule, I couldn't do it anymore. I made my lowest grade in my entire degree during that time, because I switched to survival mode. I put myself on a pace I couldn't sustain, and instead of it making me better (thriving), I was doing all I could to hang on (surviving).

I didn't pace myself.

You will be more successful in the long term if you pace yourself today, putting aside whatever anyone else is doing. This part is about you.

CAVEAT, PART 2: MAYBE IT WOULD BE BETTER IF YOU WERE DYING

I'll admit, when I stumbled upon this one, it caught me off guard.

In the book, *The Cloud of Unknowing*, the author (who, ironically is unknown) says that whether your prayer time is short or long, "the best thing you can do when you start to pray is to tell yourself, and mean it, that you're going to die at the end of your prayer."[19]

Well, I tried it. There's nothing like imminent death to change things for you. But I don't suggest doing this every day. Death can be exhausting.

However, it does open the lid to my second caveat. And that is: think short but plan long. When you think about the *value* of today, without excusing the *consequences* of tomorrow, you're in the sweet spot. This allows you to be completely present and not wasting time—because who knows if you'll live to tomorrow. But it also allows you to not inherit a mess if tomorrow does arrive.

Joel Gunz, writer and self-declared Alfred Hitchcock "geek," used to be a Jehovah's Witness. In a Medium.com article, he tells what it was like living at the end of the world.

In October of 1975, faithful Witnesses were once again preparing for the end of the world. In the years leading up to it, "some of our friends sold their houses to go preach in faraway lands. Witness youths [sic] dropped out of school to devote their remaining time in this old world to the ministry. Yet others treated themselves to spendy vacations, because—why not? —their credit card debt was soon to go up in smoke."[20]

This is a sad example of what happens when you get off-kilter and slide to an extreme. And while extreme, it's not that uncommon.

Jesus gave us the other end of this spectrum. He told the story of a divided bridal party. First-century Jewish custom had the bridesmaids waiting at the house for the bride and groom to arrive. As this all happened after dark, the bridesmaids had torches with oil to keep them alight.

Half of the bridesmaids weren't prepared and didn't bring enough oil. Their lamps died in the middle of it all, so they had to run back home and get more oil. The other half anticipated the delay and brought extra oil. And the ones who planned ahead were the only ones there when the bride and groom rolled up. When the others came back, the party had moved on.

The moral of this last caveat: live for today while planning for tomorrow. I know that's obvious-sounding.

But if you look around, it's clear this is not something our culture values. Planning for tomorrow gets plenty of lip service. But living for today is the ubiquitous message of advertisements and self-help books alike. It's an upstream swim, but it's what keeps us from sliding into one of those dangerous extremes.

Speaking of balance, the next chapter takes an outside-in approach. Disciplining yourself is one thing, but getting the rest of life on board is another thing entirely.

NOTES

[1] Goleman, Daniel, *Focus* (HarperCollins, 2013), 4.

[2] Ibid., 4.

[3] http://www.foxnews.com/leisure/2016/03/02/chick-fil-offers-free-ice-cream-for-customers-who-put-away-their-phones/, accessed July 26, 2016.

[4] On iPhone you can do this one-by-one in Notifications in the Settings app. And since Android tends to precede iPhone in almost everything, I'm sure you can do something similar there, too.

[5] Cloud, Henry, *Changes That Heal* (Zondervan, 2003), 111.

[6] Goleman, Daniel, *Focus* (HarperCollins, 2013), 21.

[7] Ibid., 22.

[8] Consider, for a few: Psalm 63:1, 68:4-5, 71:8, 103:1, 105:1, 143:6, and 150:6.

[9] Some people call this journaling, but others (me) are squeamish about that title.

[10] Consider abortion. This is directly against Christian morality (murder). Yet lobbyists fight for it to be both legal and compulsive (e.g. healthcare provisional requirements). If Pro-Choice (pro-abortion) lobbyists win governmental support, then Pro-Life (anti-abortion) supporters are forced to comply against their beliefs. This is a morality that has become legislated. Yet many of this same Pro-Choice camp claim the opposite of their actions. Take another

example, the LGBTQ debate. Christian morality stipulates marriage is only between one man and one woman. Yet, the LGBTQ cause fights to change this. It has then become 'wrong' for Christians to keep their definition and not adopt this new definition. But why? This is nothing more than the forcing of one's opinions and beliefs onto another.

[11] Lewis, C.S., *Mere Christianity* (HarperCollins, 2001).

[12] See Genesis 1:27 and James 3:9.

[13] https://www.census.gov/population/www/cen2000/censusatlas/pdf/10_Education.pdf, accessed July 27, 2016.

[14] McGonigal, Kelly, *The Willpower Instinct* (Penguin Group, 2012), 24.

[15] Ibid., 25.

[16] Two great books on this are F.F. Bruce's *The New Testament Documents* and Gary Habermas' *The Historical Jesus*.

[17] As I write this I am again enrolled in school, doing some post-grad work. The "past all that" comment is a reference to the K-12 grades which are almost all compulsory in the US and fall into a different category entirely from college, grad school, or any other 'elective' type of learning.

[18] Foster, Richard, *Celebration of Discipline* (HarperSanFransisco, 1998), 63.

[19] Unknown Author, *The Cloud Of Unknowing*, Edited by Richard Foster and Emile Griffin, *Spiritual Classics* (HarperSanFrancisco, 2000), 43-44.

[20] https://medium.com/bigger-picture/the-jehovahs-witness-who-knew-too-much-a93898efd64#.4yo73mso4, accessed July 29, 2016.

chapter five

FOR THE NEXT 20 MINUTES

"Pay mind to your own life, your own health, and wholeness.
A bleeding heart is of no help to anyone
if it bleeds to death."
- Frederick Buechner

S ometimes there's a balance that life gives us all on its own. Things just work. But, most of the time, at least in my case, that's not the way it is. I remember one day lying on my own couch next to my wife when the truth hit me. "Kristin, I don't do 'balance' very well."

After a year of being married to me and without looking up from her magazine, she replied, "I know."

For me, the problem is a lack of moderation. When I like something, I love it. And when I'm tired of something else, I'd just as soon throw it away.

Habit and behavioral researchers frequently weigh in on this, because, as I mentioned in the chapter on willpower, having a balanced life is important to making and keeping good habits. It's all a flow that moves together.

One of those components is physical exercise. If you live in America—not to slight America—you probably already know: exercise is good, but we need more of it.

And I've been down this track before. I get fired up to "get back in shape," and then pretty soon I'm logging my morning run times, mapping out my neighborhood route (to increase my distance incrementally, of course), all the while listening to podcasts about how to be a better runner (not kidding).

Until that is, it quietly (and usually over night) fades to nothing. After a short while, I lose interest because I've invested *way* too much time and energy into this stuff. And I'm back at square one thinking I need to get myself in shape.

That is until I learned about the 20-minute rule.

New York Times columnist and health researcher Gretchen Reynolds explains that 20 minutes of physical activity is the magic number for staying healthy.

"You should walk or otherwise work out lightly," writes Reynolds, "for 150 minutes a week in order to improve your health."[1] That's not running per se. That's just walking enough to get your blood circulating. One hundred and fifty minutes comes to about 20 minutes per day.

And here's an interesting finding: how you split that up doesn't make a big difference. You can do 50 minutes three times a week, or 20 minutes every day. The result is the same.[2]

But what *is* the result?

According to a University of Cambridge meta-analysis, "in general a person's risk of dying prematurely from any cause plummeted by nearly 20 percent if he or she" followed this 150 minute-per-week guideline.[3]

For me this was great. It gave me the rationale to squeeze the necessary amount of physical exercise into my day, and to do it in a way I could maintain over the long haul.

That gave me a good framework, but what kind of exercise?

"The body gets used to a certain level of activity with impressive rapidity," writes Reynolds. "So you have to ratchet things up."[4] But ratcheting up isn't a deal-breaker. Often changing your type of workout or the amount of time you do it is enough. In fact, "as a general rule, you shouldn't increase your training volume by much more than 10 percent a week, to avoid injury."[5]

One way to do this is to increase the intensity. The 20 minutes a day is referring to light work. But "six minutes or so a week of hard exercise (plus the time spent warming up, cooling down, and resting between the bouts of intense work) [has] proven to be as good as about three hundred minutes of less strenuous exercise for achieving basic fitness."[6]

In 20 minutes you can get the exercise you need to stay healthy, which keeps you living longer, all the while developing the kind of structure that makes habit formation successful.

Excellent.

Now, let's move on to why sugar is good.

SWEET LIKE BUTTER

It shouldn't come as much of a surprise that we in America eat too much sugar. "Sugar-Busters" and other low- or no-carb plans like "Atkins" or the "South Beach" diet are all about getting your sugar, or carb, intake down to zero in some cases. Weight loss is a convoluted problem because our bodies are so good at maintaining the status quo. Taking this all together, there's a regular narrative that sugar is bad.

And too much sugar *is* bad.

But so is too much milk, and too much meat, and too much water, and anything else you over-do. When it comes to food, moderation is healthy. The general criticism of some of these diets is that they take their methods to an unhealthy extreme, though that is a hotly debated topic.

But back to sugar. Sometimes we believe a certain way, and then researchers are able to show us something we didn't expect. "Sugars help you to exercise better," writes Reynolds. Sugar or carbs are energy, and so this makes sense. But "at the same time nature is fair about these things, exercise also helps your body to deal with any health impacts from ingesting" too much sugar.[7]

Eating right is about balance and moderation. The British United Provident Association recommends a third of your diet be starchy foods, another third fruits and vegetables, and the balance be split between dairy and non-dairy protein, with about five percent for sugars and fats.[8] While the specifics will vary, the idea is to keep it balanced.

Balance works because—as I've been saying all along—we are holistic beings. When our body is fighting an infection, our minds get sluggish because it pulls resources.

When we're under a lot of stress at work, it shows up in aches and pains in our lower back and neck. And what we eat affects our mood and our energy, which in turn affects how much physical activity we get.

When you're trying to start a new habit, or kill an old one, focusing solely on that habit is like walking through a minefield without a map. You *might* make it. But to be successful, you need to think about the *whole* picture. Your physical activity and your diet are as important as the rest.

And speaking of success, I have become a new convert in another area.

SECRET SLEEP

Our culture praises those who sleep less and push through without taking a rest. Taking a vacation is acceptable—as long as you stay connected and, well, don't stop working. And on normal days, answering emails into the night is not only acceptable, it's *expected*.

But is this really good? Are we actually more productive like this?

Sleep researcher and neuroscientist at the University of Manchester, Penelope Lewis, says "no." And not by a long shot. "In many ways, a sleep-deprived brain," writes Lewis, "acts like a brain under the influence of alcohol."[9]

But inebriation is not a perfect analogy. Sleep deprivation seems to affect "only the most complex tasks—those requiring creativity, lateral thinking, innovation, and flexibility."[10] And "surprisingly, high-level processes that require logical deduction, such as IQ tests and critical reasoning, are performed more or less normally even after *two full nights* without sleep."[11] So it's very possible that we live sleep-deprived, do fine in some areas, and assume all is okay.

But there's more. Sleep deprivation also causes people to engage in riskier behavior than they normally do and "also appears to impair moral judgments."[12]

These are the negative effects of not getting enough sleep. But these weren't what eventually moved me to change my habits. It wasn't until I understood what my body needed sleep *for* (the positive case), that I became an ambassador of sleep.

Sleep is when the brain cleans itself out. Neuroscientists call this *synaptic homeostasis*. This is the way it works: Throughout the day your brain is making hundreds of thousands and even millions of connections (called synapses). This is how you process and understand the world. Some of these connections are helpful, some aren't, and others are just plain distracting. So after a full day, your brain needs to unwind, or "downscale." "This downscaling not only makes space for new learning, [but] it also removes noise and…increases the ratio between important information and [useless] noise."[13] In other words, sleep is cleaning up after the crazy party that was your day.

But the value of sleep goes beyond day-to-day brain-cleaning. "Sleeping may actually turn out to be one of the most proactive ways you could possibly try to solve whatever problem is bothering you," writes Lewis.[14]

This works because of "the general principle that neurons which fire together wire together," as we saw in chapter one. The more you associate certain things, the more they become a trigger for each other. During your nightly mental cleaning, your brain clears out all the noise leaving the stronger connections as often "the only thing that is retained."[15]

So far, so good, but being a pragmatist, my next battlefield was one of efficiency. What does making up sleep really look like, and how does that work?

Unfortunately, most researchers find that you *can't* catch up on your sleep. At least not in a way that's meaningful. While *some* side-effects can be negated if you sleep extra in the next few days, most can't. The best plan is to get the right amount of sleep each night, and when you miss that, to either take a nap during the day, or get back to your proper amount as soon as you can.[16]

***

Most people, generally speaking, are morning people. But most people also don't get enough sleep, and so it's not terribly apparent that they are their best in the morning. One of the strongest assets you have in life is getting enough sleep. It took me about six months of unscientific trial and error to figure out how much sleep is good for me. I used to get six (sometimes five) hours a night because I was trying to maximize my day. But then I learned that getting the right amount of sleep not only makes me feel better, but *it's* what makes my day more productive. Now I get between seven and eight hours a night. And for most people, the seven-to-nine range is healthy.

I'm also a morning person, so that's when I do my prayer time. But my wife most certainly *isn't*, and so she does all this stuff at night. There's no right or wrong here. You should focus on what's most natural for you. If you're better in the morning, then let that be your time for prayer and reading your Bible. Or if you come alive at night (bless you), then make that your time. To get started, I suggest *not* picking a time during the middle of the day. This can be done effectively, but it's rarely easy and often takes more discipline. Always make the first step the easiest.

THE LAW OF WATER

This is a paradigm, or a change in thought, more than it is a change in physique.

Many moons ago Aristotle coined the principle that water seeks its own level. When you spill your drink, it goes down and spreads out. I know that's not exactly a revelation. But its implications are helpful for understanding why it can be so hard to change habits.

When we stop doing something, there's the very real possibility we'll start back again. Just like water spreading out and filling the void, when we stop doing something and don't replace that time or activity with something else, then our wiring naturally moves back to autopilot, which is the action it was previously doing.

One way to look at this is how behaviorist James Clear explains it. "Because bad habits provide some type of benefit in your life [like curing boredom or relieving stress], it's very difficult to simply eliminate them...

Instead, you need to replace a bad habit with a new habit that provides a similar benefit."[17]

This explains why it's so hard to quit looking at email in the evening or when you're on vacation. Neurologically, getting a new email is a reward, so we're motivated to check often, hoping for more rewards.

Part of the solution for curbing this when we're off-duty is to remove the cue (see chapter two) by turning off notifications after hours or even putting your phone out of sight. But this doesn't always work. At least not for me. I'll still think about my phone and go find it to check. What then?

Next stop: change the reward. For me, the promise of an email is some new piece of interesting information. So when I'm trying to relax and think I might be likely to reach for the phone, I keep an interesting book on hand. This is not something for research or work, it's purely something I'm interested in (like with the Oreos). There's always some amount of willpower needed, but by removing the cue and supplementing the reward, I'm much more likely to be able to succeed on willpower.

The Law of Water is a reminder to always fill the void.

SPIRITUAL GLUTTONY

In 1 Thessalonians 5:16, Paul says we are to "pray without ceasing." But praying *constantly* is not what Paul meant. Jesus didn't pray constantly. When He went up on the mountain to pray (Matthew 14:23), or before His execution when He went to a place in the garden by Himself to pray (Matthew 26:36), we're seeing examples when He *initiated* a time of prayer. He wasn't already praying. He began to pray at these times. So, not only would a constant state of prayer be unrealistic (and I would add to that, impossible), it would be *beyond* the example of Jesus.

Instead, what Paul is saying is to always stay in touch with God. We shouldn't cordon off areas of our life that we don't share with God, and we shouldn't put ourselves in positions where we can't pray, like doing something deliberately against the Spirit's leading or teaching. This is what it means to "pray without ceasing."

To survive in the long run, and to have a healthy spiritual life, there are certain boundaries we must put in place. Even boundaries in our spiritual disciplines. Richard Foster, who wrote one of the best modern books on the spiritual disciplines, writes, "Practicality is a special grace to us, for everyone who takes the ministry of prayer serious is sorely tempted toward spiritual gluttony. Rest and play and good conversations are proper complements to the work of prayer."[18]

There's absolutely no shame in having a relaxing time off, even if it's during your normal prayer time. The reality is that you will occasionally need a break, and that will involve doing something relaxing. Even in the 10 Commandments, the fourth was to take a break.

There is a very real temptation that as we strive for excellence, we can do it at the peril of our own health and longevity. This kind of intensity has the pseudo-feeling of dedication. But it's really just the predecessor to burn-out.

Jesus said man was not made for the Sabbath, but the Sabbath for man (Mark 2:23-28). Meaning the priority is on the health of our relationship with God. All the rules are meant to support that.

ALL TOGETHER NOW

What do exercise, sugar, and sleep have to do with the spiritual disciplines?

Simply put, everything. I'll say it again: we're holistic beings. Everything we do affects another part of us. I've mentioned this before, but it helps to keep beating this stick because thinking like this is what makes these changes stick in our lives.

Here's an example of what this is like. Think of a bucket with holes in it. It's going to be hard (but not impossible) to fill that up. One way is to pour in water faster. If you can put in water faster than it leaks out through the holes, then you might be able to fill it up. Of course, as soon as you stop pouring in water, it'll all drain out, and your bucket will be empty again. (Not to mention, your floor will be soaked.)

What's the better way? Plug the holes. But that takes some time. And at first it doesn't feel productive (the bucket's still empty during the hole-filling process). But when you do begin to pour in water, it's notably different. Your floor isn't soaked, for one. But there also becomes a time when you can *stop* pouring in water. It fills up. In other words, addressing the holes first is a plan that works.

Focusing on only one or two areas of our lives while ignoring the rest is like trying to fill a bucket with holes in it. It's possible (sometimes), but it's hardly the best way. And most of the time, it just ends in frustration. Instead, the better way is to look at our life as a whole.[19] When we do this, we can pinpoint the areas that will cause us to fail —areas that often aren't directly connected (like how much sleep we're getting, or how our diet is affecting our mood). Thinking holistically, or all together, is what it takes to make these new disciplines not only stick, but work.

NOTES

[1] Reynolds, Gretchen, *The First 20 Minutes* (Hudson Street Press, 2012), 8.

[2] Ibid., 7.

[3] Ibid., 9.

[4] Ibid., 10.

[5] Ibid., 10.

[6] Ibid., 13.

[7] Ibid., 57.

[8] http://www.bupa.co.uk/health-information/directory/h/healthy-eating, accessed July 20, 2016.

[9] Lewis, Penelope A., *The Secret World of Sleep* (Palgrave MacMillan, 2013), 16.

[10] Ibid., 18.

[11] Ibid., 19. Emphasis mine.

[12] Ibid., 19.

[13] Ibid., 50-52.

[14] Ibid., 101.

[15] Ibid., 109.

[16] Consider "Can You Ever REALLY Catch-up on Sleep" on Psychology Today, https://www.psychologytoday.com/blog/sleep-newzzz/201311/can-you-ever-really-catch-sleep, accessed July 20, 2016. And: "You Can't 'Catch Up On Sleep'" from the National Sleep Foundation, https://sleepfoundation.org/sleep-news/you-cant-catch-sleep, accessed July 20, 2016.

[17] http://jamesclear.com/how-to-break-a-bad-habit, accessed July 19, 2016

[18] Foster, Richard, Emilie Griffin (Editors), Spiritual Classics (HarperSanFrancisco, 2000), 41.

[19] That's borderline punny, I know. I didn't do it on purpose, but I'm owning it now.

chapter six

A PLACE TO GO

"We know that without food we would die.
Without fellowship,
life is not worth living."
- Laurie Colwin

"I'm a reflection of the community."
- Tupac Shakur

For many, church has taken on the concept of a spectator sport—I go for what I get out of it, not what I give to it. But this is backward. If you go to church for what you can *get* out of it, then the sermon will be lacking and the people will be irritating. (Trust me.)

But if you switch that; if you go for the purpose of *giving*, then something ironic happens. You feel full. In essence, by giving, you will feel as if you've been given to.

This is because of a simple principle. When Jesus came as a man to live with us, and then die for us, it was out of love. Love is not a mushy emotion (though it sometimes produces that), instead, it's a protective action.

When Jesus did die for us, it didn't take him billions of times. It took him just once, because love is not a finite resource, it's an infinite one. His love and his sacrifice work for everyone who has chosen to give up their way and follow his.

So when we give, we are stepping into this same stream. It's not something we're responsible *for*, like a paycheck. It's more something we're responsible *with*—a thing entrusted to us. Before leaving, Jesus gave us all one last direction—go everywhere and teach them all that I've done for you. And if they choose it, I'll do it for them, too.

***

Being involved in a local church is one of the single greatest opportunities we have. I'm not selling seats here. I just believe this to be completely true.

I've heard countless times that the church is full of hypocrites. And that's true. I'm a hypocrite. And so are you —we all are. Are we really looking to be involved in a group of pristine strangers? Or rather real people with real problems?

There will be plenty of people in church who have the wrong mindset—people driven by what they can get out of it, instead of what they can put into it. But that's to be expected. We live in a pretty messed up place.

The reason the very last thing Jesus told us to do was "make disciples" was because that's the very thing this world *needs* us to do.

And so we connect with each other to strengthen, teach, learn, encourage, and support one another. *That's* what church is actually about.

SPIRITUALLY SOCIAL

Being social in our spiritual lives means connecting with others on a spiritual level. This is an action.

Several places in the New Testament talk about spiritual gifts.[1] These are the things God has given us to further the kingdom. Our gifts are not our tasks. When God puts something on your heart to do, it may be in line with a gifting you have, or it may not be. But our giftings are the things that naturally make sense to us.

The word gifts might be a bit misleading. Gifts are not fully formed skills—they're more like desires planted in our hearts.

For me, my gifts are teaching and encouragement. It's funny, as I look back now, these things are undeniable, though I didn't always know these were mine. The way I discovered them was just by doing what felt right. For as long as I can remember, I have always desired to make others feel encouraged. And the same for teaching. I can recount many embarrassing things now, but it's only because I was doing what my heart drove me to.

Through practice and experience we learn to hone the gifts we have been given. And we use these gifts when we come together, in tandem, as the body of Christ, unified around Jesus' message of hope.

WHEN YOU'VE GOT RHYTHM

In all of this, in the spiritual disciplines, the intention is to get into a rhythm and make this a living and breathing part of your life. I heard this saying one time, "there are five Gospels: Matthew, Mark, Luke, John, and you. And most people will only ever read the fifth one." People read us by watching us.

Your prayer time doesn't have to be rigid. And, honestly, it doesn't have to be terribly consistent. It can have variety. The heart behind it all is to get the things of God under your skin. Not in an irritating way, but in a permeating way. When your life is conformed to God and His ways, then the details will take care of themselves.

When you find yourself making progress in this direction, your prayer time will start to feel like a boat carried in a stream. You'll still need to stick your oars in from time to time, to keep it all on track, but most of the forward motion is a result of where you are. When Paul tells us to pray without ceasing, this is the rhythm he's talking about.

Some mornings I pray for over an hour. Other mornings only ten minutes. Some mornings I'm praying about something that directly feeds into my writing, and with a flash of inspiration I get up mid-thought and immediately start writing. Other mornings, I feel a bit stuck, and I don't feel like I'm making any traction. And other mornings still, I wake up late or do something altogether different. The point is that after a while, it will not be a legalistic matter, but will instead become a natural flow.

I believe the kind of life God wants for us is one that includes Him in *all* aspects of it, not just a specific prayer time. We should be able to flow from one thing to another, throughout our day, with God being the common denominator to them all. He might not be actively on our thoughts, but neither should He be far from them.

THE WHOLE BOOK IN 30 SECONDS

In case you missed it, here's a replay of the book.

Our brains are built as a highly organized system of highways. What comes out is largely a result of what we put in. And despite our best efforts, it's rarely a process we can manipulate.

The things we do (habits) consist of a three-part cycle: a cue, a routine, and a reward. When we want to start or change a habit, our best bet is to focus first on the cue. That's the part that gets the rest started. And if the reward is something you're excited about, you'll have a better chance of getting the new or changed habit to stick.

While this sounds simple, it's only half of the battle. Our surroundings play a big part in our success, because, while willpower is needed to get things rolling, it's not strong enough to sustain long term change. For that, we need enough elements of our environment on board. That includes everything from what we see, to our schedule and the friends we hang out with.

Focusing is the heart of this book. While I don't go into the spiritual disciplines themselves, I do talk about the number one tool needed to apply them: focus. Here I offer three tactics summed up in three words: deep, wide, and forward.

And just like habit formation is not a singular activity, neither is focusing. Our success depends on our staying healthy, both physically and emotionally.

Lastly, and as a natural progression of the last thought, we need to be spiritually healthy too. This cannot be done except in a community.

THE END

This book was a combination of neurological and behavioral science, as well as my own experiments. The question was: how can we use the tools God's already given us, to get better at building our lives around him? That's what this book sought to answer.

I footnoted everything that wasn't my own, which you can see at the end of each chapter. If you're curious to learn more, feel free to use these footnotes as a guide. I sourced from only the best of my research.

If you have questions or would like to chat more, feel free to reach out. My email is ajoefontenot@gmail.com.

And if you'd like to get more resources like this, visit JoeFontenot.info.

P.S.

If this book helped you better understand how to change your behavior, and gave you some ideas about what you can start doing to create a stronger prayer time, then please leave a review for it on Amazon.com.

NOTES

[1] See Romans 12, 1 Corinthians 12, and Ephesians 4.

ACKNOWLEDGMENTS

This is the part most people usually skip. But after having written a book, I think this is probably the most important part. Nothing like this is done in a vacuum.

As such, I am grateful to everyone who has weighed in and helped me create this, but specially: Kristin, Stacey, David, Hiram, Rich, Sam, Travis, and Jim.

All mistakes still here are, unmistakably, my own.

ABOUT THE AUTHOR

Joe is the marketing strategist for one of the largest seminaries in the world. And through his company, Five Round Rocks, he helps entrepreneurs and nonprofits create smart marketing. Before this, he worked in international logistics, helping NGOs move humanitarian aid cargo all over the world.

He and his wife and their two kids recently relocated to the mountains of East Tennessee.

NONFICTION BOOKS

A Year of Sabbaths (2018)
This is a companion to *Life Hacking Spiritual Disciplines*.
Getting started is hard. And so I created a super-short
devotional, designed to be used one day a week. It's a too-
easy-not-to-try sort of thing.

Minimalist Marketing (2018)
This book steps more into my professional career. It's
designed for entrepreneurs and nonprofits — people who
often don't have a lot of money to spend on ads or

marketing teams. It begins with the key principles of successful marketing (strategies), and then it moves on to specific and common applications (tactics).

Aphoring (2020)
A book I wrote for my kids about navigating life — including a few of the lessons I've learned along the way.

FICTION BOOKS
Written as A.J. Fontenot

The Golden Chair (2019)
This was my first novel. And for the most part, the reviews have been great. It's Book One of a trilogy. The story is about Erin Reed, a former journalist, who is investigating her mother's mysterious death, which happened a quarter of a century ago. The truth, she finds, is more dangerous than she realized…

The Century Man (2020)
This is book 2 in the Erin Reed trilogy. It takes Erin down to Colombia, in South America — a country I was able to visit a couple years before.

The Vesper File (2020)

This is the final book in the Erin Reed trilogy, bringing everything to a conclusion. Well, mostly.

OTHER RESOURCES

5 Step Guide to Get the Most Out of Your Daily Prayer Time

This is very short PDF you can download and print off. It walks through a practical framework for not getting distracted when you sit down to read and pray. You can find it at PracticalSpiritualGrowth.tools, or at JoeFontenot.info/prayer-guide

Made in the USA
Middletown, DE
19 February 2021